Piper Learns Others Can Too

ALEXIS THOMPSON

PAGE PUBLISHING
Conneaut Lake, PA

First originally published by Page Publishing 2024

ISBN 979-8-89157-391-8 (pbk)
ISBN 979-8-89157-407-6 (digital)

Printed in the United States of America

To anyone who has ever felt *different*.

GOOD
DAY!!
GLUE
PAPER

Piper Dan's favorite part of school was making new friends. She especially loved helping them.

In class, a girl named Rae reached into a cabinet for a stick of glue. Rae only had one hand, and Piper could tell reaching was hard for her.
GLUE
PASTE
CR
PAPER
PAPER

"Here, I can grab that for you," Piper said, stepping up to grab it. She frowned. She couldn't reach it either. "I'll go get the teacher."
GLUE
PASTE
CRAYON
CRAYON
PIPER

GLUE
ASTE
CRAYON
CRAYON
PAPER

"I can get it on my own. I appreciate the help, though," Rae said, stepping on a stool and grabbing the glue stick. Piper watched with wide eyes as Rae hopped down easily. "See, I just have to do things a little differently than you do."

Piper nodded her head. Rae was right. She could get it herself.

At lunch, Piper saw another student, Jeremy, who looked like they were going to run into a wall.

She jumped up to help. "Here, I can bring you to your seat."

"That's okay. I can do it myself," Jeremy said. "My cane helps me figure out where I'm going and keeps me from running into things."

"That's pretty cool," Piper said, watching as he swiped the cane back and forth, tapping it against tables and walls. Every time he did, he moved over a little more so he didn't hit anything.

Jeremy smiled. "It helps me do the same things that you do."

When he sat down at his table without her help, Piper saw that he was right.

The best part of the day was recess. Piper walked up to Marcus on the playground and asked if he wanted to play. He didn't answer her. So she asked if he wanted to swing. No answer.

Finally, she asked if they wanted to talk. Still no answer.

Annoyed, Piper huffed over to the teacher. "Marcus won't talk to me."

The teacher smiled at Piper. "Marcus doesn't talk."

Piper blinked, surprised. "So how does he tell you what he wants?"

"He uses pictures, notes, and sign language to communicate," the teacher said. "Why don't you try this?"

The teacher handed Piper a sheet of paper with pictures of toys on it. "This will help?"

"Definitely."

Piper skips back over to Marcus and holds up the sheet of paper. "Which one would you like to play with?" Immediately, Marcus tapped his finger on a picture of blocks and Piper smiled.

"Awesome choice."

The two built blockhouses and castles until it was time to go back inside.

DAISY

When Piper's mom picked her up from school, she asked Piper what she learned at school. Piper said, "I learned that just because someone is different, it doesn't mean they can't do everything I can."

About the Author

Alexis is a school counselor in southern California. She is a graduate of Simpson University in Redding, California, and the University of Southern California. Since starting her career, she has worked to help students know that they are heard and seen and that they are not alone. Alexis enjoys experiencing all that Southern California has to offer like attending sporting events, going to the beach, and Disneyland.